# GARY ABLETT

# GARY
# ABLETT

IRONBARK LEGENDS

First published 1996 in Ironbark by Pan Macmillan Australia Pty Limited
St Martins Tower, 31 Market Street, Sydney

Reprinted 1996

National Library of Australia
cataloguing-in-publication data:

Gary Ablett.

ISBN 0 330 35864 2.

1. Ablett, Gary. 2. Australian football players – Biography.
(Series: Ironbark Legends).

796.336092

Designed by Mark Thacker, Big Cat Design
Printed in Australia by McPherson's Printing Group

# DEDICATION

I dedicate this book to my family – parents Alfred and Colleen,
my brothers Len, Geoff, Graham, Kevin and sisters Fay, Julie and
Janice. And to my children Natasha, Gary, Nathan and Alisha.
And a special thanks to the Lord Jesus Christ for his
continuing grace and mercy upon my life.

# CONTENTS

# ABLETT, FOOTBALL'S GREAT MAGICIAN

### By John Button

*John Button has been a minister in the Labor Governments of Prime Ministers Bob Hawke and Paul Keating. More importantly, he is a fanatical supporter of Geelong Football Club. And he is one of Gary Ablett's most loyal fans.*

The worst position to find yourself in during a football game is having to head back into the play if the pass is too high. Thankfully, with the likes of Paul Couch delivering the ball, it doesn't happen too often. Here, my opponent is Matthew Febey of Melbourne in 1994.

**Y**ou catch a glimpse of him on television, umpiring a football match on the moonscape island of Nauru. He's been seen surfing at Byron Bay. He's said to be a good tennis player. At the MCG he faces up to professionals, including Test players, makes 19 runs and takes two wickets. He does a couple of rounds with the champion boxer Lester Ellis and steps from the ring with a smile on his face. He likes the bush and fishing. . . one suspects a contemplative man. The *Sunday Age* reports him in Africa on a World Vision trip, rescuing on foot a couple and their three children, trapped by torrential rain and mud in a lion-infested game park. Asked to talk about this experience he says, 'I'm sorry, I can't comment on that.'

Describing these exploits on a chat show or in the pub, a bullshit artist could turn himself into something of a legendary figure. There's a hint of a Hemingway character to build on, perhaps a touch of a Renaissance man. Gary Ablett, who has done these things, doesn't comment. He's reticent, unassuming. Fans and journalists seek him here, there and everywhere. He seems as enigmatic and elusive as the Scarlet Pimpernel. He retains, like the Latin Mass, a sense of mystery.

As a football player, Ablett is less mysterious. The goals are on the board. When he plays, the turnstiles tick over faster. Songwriters invoke the spirit of balmy September days with 'Ablett's in the air' and the 'Man we all can believe in'. He's patient with kids who clamour for his autograph. Videos sell like hot cakes. Commentators vie with each other to summon words and phrases from the deep. He's the greatest, a freak, the magician, a legend.

**(opposite) The second worst position in football is landing on your neck, which I have managed to do here against Melbourne in Round 15, 1993.**
**(below) The worst feeling in football is fronting up to the media after losing. I faced the music after our Grand Final loss in 1989.**

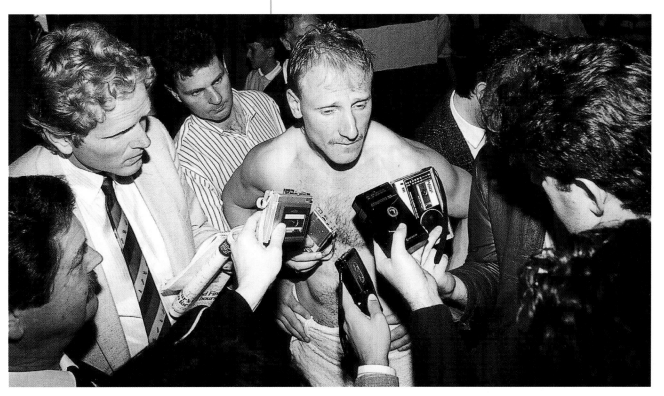

It's the word 'magician' which fits best. It captures something other players can't do. He has all the conventional skills of a champion footballer. It's the other things: the one-handed marks in a tight tussle, the spectacular leaps, the uncanny judgment and the ability to do the unexpected which make the crowd gasp. And this is the art of the magician.

I have droll memories of unexpected incidents. In 1989 the MCG was in bad shape and part of the surface was covered in thick sand. I remember Ablett racing towards goal from the half-forward flank into the pocket under the big scoreboard. A Collingwood player was in hot pursuit. 'Oh no,' said the man standing next to me, 'he's going to bounce the ball in the sand.' And he did. Twice. The man put his head in his hands. 'I've seen the lot,' he said.

Magicians are human. Occasionally they drop an egg, or a mouse pops out of a pocket when it's not supposed to. The football magician has his ups and downs: good moments and bad.

When he charges through a pack of players, you sometimes wonder whether he's in control or just hoping for the best: a good bounce or an opponent's fumble. At a crucial moment he can fall over, losing the ball or making a brilliant recovery. You hold your breath wondering which way it will go.

The magic and the mystery go together. This magician doesn't give too many secrets away. A good trick or a freak goal sometimes results in a grin; a bad kick produces a dissatisfied shake of the head. He makes enigmatic comments. A game is a game. He looks forward to the next one. 'How do you like playing in the wet?' I asked him anxiously before a game on a sodden MCG. 'Well,' he said, 'you've got to remember it's a winter sport.' I reflected on this answer for some time. It seemed philosophical rather than informative. It's also a professional's answer. A professional accepts all the rules and conditions. There are no excuses.

For over a decade Geelong supporters have had a good bargain. There have been two spectacles for the price of one. They go to see their team play and they go to see Ablett. They get, as it were, the double chance. If the team plays below form the chance is that Ablett will kick six or seven goals. He kicked 14 once in a

(opposite) Australian Football crowds are unlike any other in sport. They are loud, they know their footy, and they just love a banner.
(above) With teammates (from left) Ben Graham, Leigh Colbert and Brad Sholl, I join Geelong before the playing of the national anthem at the 1995 Grand Final against Carlton. The Blues were on song, we were not.

We have just beaten Carlton by 36 points at
Waverley Park to end the Blues eight-game
winning streak. It was also my 200th game.

**(opposite) Kicking is confidence and technique. Both come under great pressure in a Grand Final. (below) One of my favourite pastimes is relaxing at home with my four children (from left) Gary Junior, Natasha, Nathan and Alisha.**

side which lost to Essendon. Sometimes he has an off day in a winning side. It's a rare occasion, like the 1995 Grand Final, when they all played below their ability. Then the crowd feels robbed. They are used to one spectacle or another.

In recent years, when the ball has been kicked into the Geelong forward line, there's almost an assumption that Ablett will get it: a certainty about the result of a contest round the goal square. A commentator like Rex Hunt calls the outcome well before 'Gazza' has the ball. In the 80s, Geelong supporters used to make this assumption about other teams' forwards, like Jason Dunstall at Hawthorn, or Peter Daicos at Collingwood. My sons used to call it the 'cult of fear'. It's nice to have it working for us.

During the period in 1991, when Gary Ablett was 'in retirement' for 12 weeks, I walked into Kardinia Park one day with the former Geelong champion and inveterate football watcher Neil Tresize. He looked despondent, down in the mouth. 'What's the matter?' I asked. 'The game's just not the same without Ablett,' he said. 'I don't enjoy it as much.' Neil Tresize has been spoilt along with the rest of us. There's the same feeling in the crowd. In Round 21 of 1995, when Ablett was involved in an incident with Footscray's Rohan Smith, the crowd went strangely quiet for the rest of the game. They feared an involuntary retirement.

Like Neil Tresize, I've been spoilt by the Geelong spectator's double chance. It has a strange effect on your behaviour. In 1988 there were rumours that Ablett was unhappy at Geelong. Another club had reportedly made him an offer. I got steamed up. With

bitter memories of the loss of Greg Williams to Sydney in 1985, I drove out early to a Geelong game at Waverley Park. I went to the AFL dining room and asked a waiter to get members of the Geelong committee out of the lunch. Three of them came out. I gave them my best imitation of a Barassi pep talk. I said, 'if you let this bloke go you've got rocks in your head. And if he does I'll tip a bucket over you every day in the Senate for the rest of the year.' They looked a bit startled. They were not accustomed to confrontation with lunatics. I doubt if it had any effect, but it made me feel good. And Ablett stayed at Geelong. Fred Wooller, a former Geelong captain, was one of the victims. He still reminds me about it with a shameless grin.

As a young teenager I was a fan of Louis Armstrong. I listened to his music and watched him on film playing at jazz concerts. The audiences seemed as exhilarated as he was, responding happily to his art. I used to think it would be wonderful to have a job like that: being an artist who made so many people happy. So I joined the school band. I was told that I would have to play the French horn. One had to begin somewhere. I played badly. In fact I was a total failure. Later I drifted into politics, which seemed a second best option.

I recall a game against Richmond at the MCG when Gary Ablett kicked 12 goals. Halfway through the last quarter one of my sons said, 'Dad, I can't remember seeing you so happy.' Thinking about it later I remembered Louis Armstrong, another spellbinding magician. When Ablett finally hangs up his boots it will be a while before Neil Tresize, and I, and thousands of others enjoy football as much as we have. 'Gazza' will bow out with heaps of plaudits and many of football's glittering prizes. I suspect the greatest satisfaction for him will be the knowledge that his talents have brought so much pleasure to so many people.

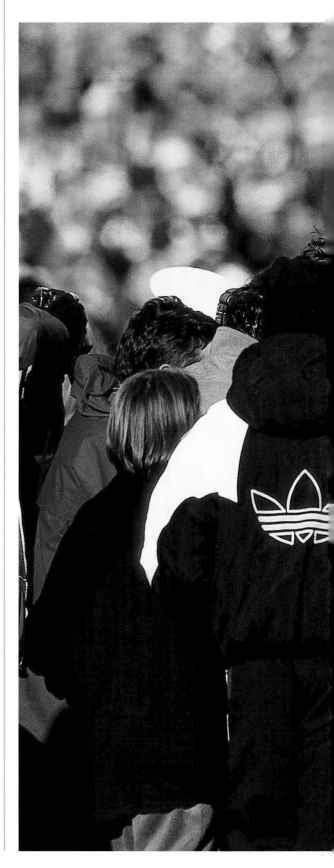

(opposite) Another of my favourite pastimes, but not my neighbours', is playing the saxophone.
(below) Booting your 100th goal for the season is a great thrill, but it always starts a stampede by fans who rush on to the ground to congratulate you. After reaching the 'ton' in 1995 I was grateful for the help from teammates, trainers and police.

It is with his feet and hands that Ablett articulates his thoughts. And, hey, we're not complaining... More than 28,000, Geelong's biggest crowd of the year turned out at Kardinia Park to watch him pass 100 goals for the third straight year. Ron Hovey, the Geelong president, was still shaking his head in amazement after the game, and he estimated that Ablett had put 10,000 on the attendance.

Martin Blake, *The Age*, 31 July 1995.

I will always be indebted to my father for ensuring that I learnt to kick with both feet. Here, I get away on the left foot from Carlton's Steve Silvagni.

15

# GROWING UP IN DROUIN

One-on-one battle with Carlton's Mil Hanna in 1994. I'm not sure if I got a free kick or not. I like to think I did.

We were a close family. With eight children and just two bedrooms we had no option. You picked on one Ablett, you picked on eight. But there were times when I tested the bond. The family grimly remembers the day they came home to find that the barn where my father stacked the hay for his horses, and where the kids plonked their bikes, had all but burnt down.

I could only have been about six at the time and I was left on my own just long enough to experiment with matches and a small amount of hay. I was no Professor Julius Sumner Miller. I suggest no-one else try such tests, rather they take it from me that it causes a fire. And quickly.

When everyone got home I was hiding under the house having done my best to douse the fire with the garden hose. When my mother caught up with me she used the hose on my bottom rather than the fire. A painful lesson.

(opposite) In football you are nothing without your teammates. After a goal against West Coast in Round 13, 1995, Paul Brown, myself and Billy Brownless vow to kick some more.

(top of page) In Drouin, there was sport and then more sport. Here, I show the spoils of a Little Athletics triumph.

(above) A proud moment. I won the best and fairest in the Under-12 competition.

(left) Walking races were big in Little Athletics at Drouin. And you can see I took them seriously.

19

**(above) The skills I learnt playing in the dusty streets of Drouin were the foundation of my game at senior level.**
**(below) Playing as a junior in the Drouin seniors was pretty serious stuff. They were tough men. Thankfully, I had my brothers on hand for a little 'peacemaking'.**

We must have been close to survive my mischief but I cannot have been too bad. My nickname up until I was about 10 was 'Noddy' because I didn't say too much. I would either nod my head for 'yes' or shake it if the answer was 'no'. I didn't mind it too much because it saved people making names up because of my legs. They were big-boned but skinny, nobbly. I always thought Noddy was going to be a better nickname than Nobbly.

My parents Alfred and Colleen shared the third bedroom of our plain weatherboard home. In my room were my older brothers Lennie, Geoff, Graham and Kevin. We had double bunks. I was on a top one. Sisters Fay, Julie and Janice shared the other bedroom. The house is still there and so are my parents. I was closest to Janice, who is one year younger than me. There is a four-year gap between myself and Kevin.

When I was about 13 my parents built a large bungalow out the back and all the boys moved in there and the girls took over our bedroom.

I think life was pretty tough for my parents. Eight kids demand a lot of work and a lot of patience. My father seemed to work from daylight to dusk to make sure we had what we needed. With eight hungry kids sitting around the dinner table we used to have to say grace with our eyes open.

I will always be grateful to my father for taking me aside when

Unbelievably, this was a goal. I think the placement of the tongue had everything to do with it.

The final moments before the 1995 Grand Final. Although you're about to play the game in front of 90,000 people, you're alone with your own thoughts and expectations. Strangely, it is a very private time as you work to control your emotions and channel them in a positive direction.

23

I was about five and teaching me to kick with my left foot. I was a natural right footer but my father insisted I learn to use both sides of my body. It wasn't easy at first but now, after 14 years in VFL/AFL football, I am so grateful my father took the interest and time.

Lennie and the other boys often get to Geelong games. My parents always do. I get back to Drouin maybe three or four times a year and it jogs the memory banks. Of the funny times, silly times. Most of my energy seems to have been spent playing sport or mucking about with mates. My earliest thoughts are falling off a big chestnut that my father had plonked me, Kevin and Graham on. It tripped and sent us tumbling off. They reckon I accidently kicked the horse but I'm sure it put its foot in a pot-hole. I was only three at the time so I don't know who to believe. It certainly turned me off horses. I only began riding again when I was in my teens, although I have never shared my father's love of horse racing itself.

It was a good time to grow up. My father was training horses and was also a cartage contractor and he would spend up to a couple of weeks at a time away from home. Sometimes you would get to go with him and camp out at night. When he was working I'd be fishing. Those days you could drop a line in the Murray and catch five nice fish in 20 minutes. Sadly, you can't do that now.

You can imagine the scenes about the house with such a sporting family. My mother still holds a few running records at her

**(above) In action against Footscray in 1994. We played Footscray three times that season, the last win coming from a Billy Brownless goal after the siren in the First Qualifying Final.**

old school in Darnum, near the Victorian town of Warragul. My father was asked to play at Carlton but the world was at war and he joined the navy instead. He was on a PT boat off Darwin during the war.

My sisters were all good netballers and all my brothers could kick a footy. The eldest was Lennie who played with Drouin and was invited down to Geelong by that great recruiter Bill McMaster.

Geoff graduated from Drouin to play 202 games with Hawthorn, 16 with Richmond and 11 with St Kilda. He was quick and regularly won the sprint during half-time at the Grand Final. Graham played six games with Hawthorn's reserves on permit. He could have been very good but he didn't have the same passion as the rest of us. Kevin played 30 games with Hawthorn as well as a handful of matches with Richmond and Geelong.

After school there would be up to 20 kids outside our house ready for a footy match. We'd pick skippers then select the sides. Being one of the youngest, I was always one of the last picked. We would do the umpiring ourselves. Drouin has produced a lot of AFL footballers but I'd reckon the count would be short on umpires. Decapitation was the only grounds for a free kick for around the neck.

We played any sport—baseball, cricket, soccer. I loved soccer nearly as much as footy and we played every other week at school. In 1989 I got to see a second division match in London but it remains a burning ambition to see a premier league match live. I never miss the soccer on television.

I vividly remember one cricket match in which we had two full sides. My brother Geoff was batting, got one a bit short and rocked on to his back foot and played a superb hook shot. Square leg didn't see it, fine leg didn't have a chance but the neighbours across the road were never going to miss it. It went straight through their front window. Funny, what I remember most is the speed at which 22 kids disappeared. As a kid I wasn't the quickest but I can tell you I gained a yard that night.

It was not the only window to be broken around Drouin as the Abletts and their mates played sport. Not everyone masters the torpedo punt first off.

It is true I lived for sport, first at Drouin State School then the High School. It is also true I didn't live for school. I wasn't too bad up to grade six but after that the school reports noticed a 'waning of interest' in the more scholarly pursuits in life. By 15 I called it quits. I worked on and off as a brickie's labourer as both my parents urged me to secure a future, but I had no real vision of what lay ahead for me.

I felt that I had no option but to leave school. I didn't enjoy it, some of the subjects I was doing felt irrelevant and I didn't get on too well with a couple of the teachers. No doubt they felt they didn't get on with me.

**(below) Here, Gary Junior takes a spectacular grab over me. Nathan waits for the crumbs.**

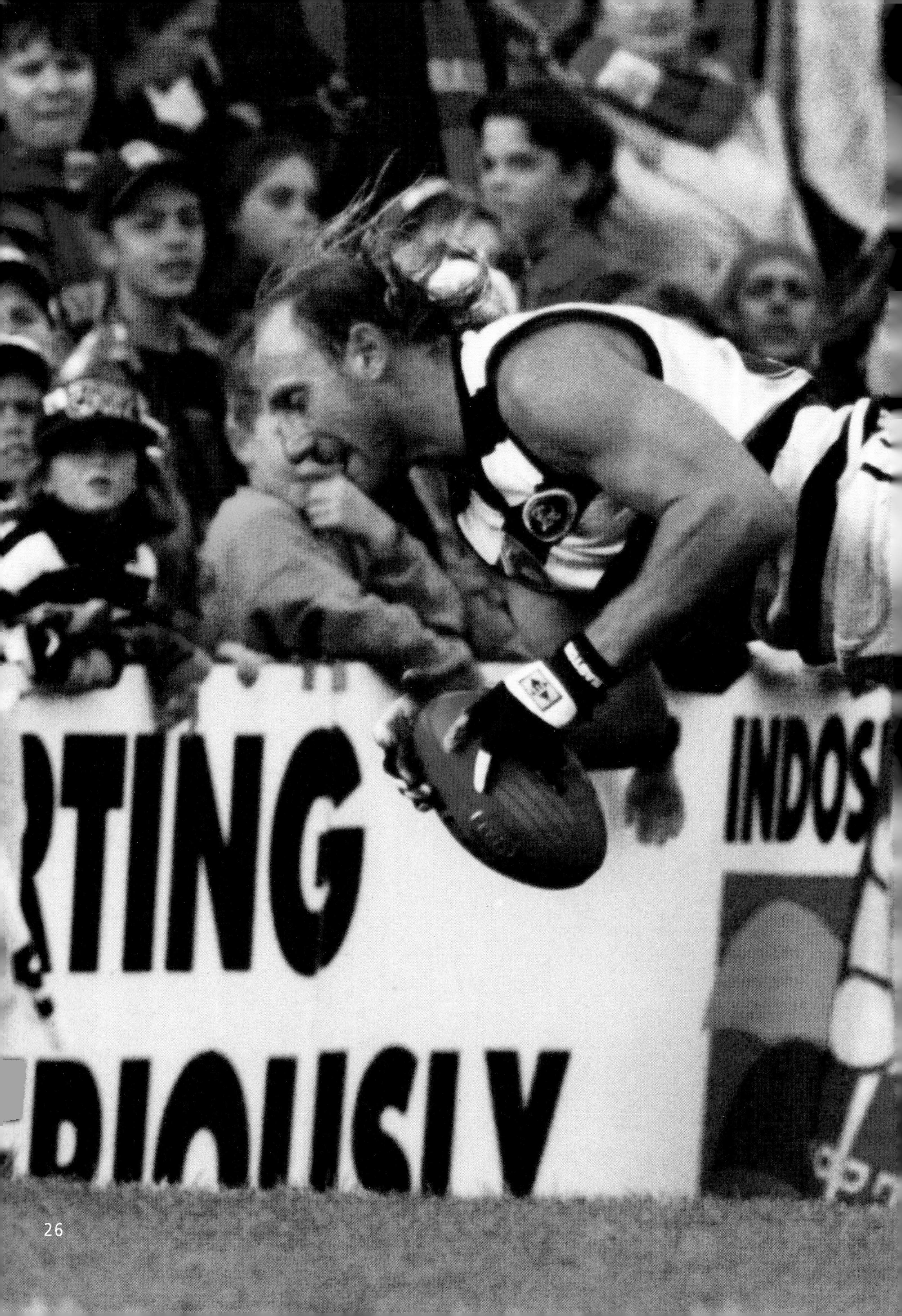
RTING
INDOS

The introduction of gloves in the early 1990s proved popular with many players, especially in wet conditions. However, they could never guarantee a soft landing.

Third from the right, second row from the front. He looks skinny and a little out of place. Around him are the thick arms and whiskered faces of the victors of Drouin, the local farmers, tradesmen and truck drivers, tough men who could cop a knock and keep on going.

He sits there, arms crossed, staring at the camera with the rest of his teammates. He is just 16, with a body still growing, but already Gary Ablett has earned his place in a world of older, tougher men. Already, they have seen the way he positions his young body, the uncanny knack of reading the flight of the ball and his ability to kick improbable goals.

So, too, have the scouts from the Victorian Football League. They were thick on the ground in 1978, for word had already passed around that up in the bush a kid called Gary Ablett was showing something special. Here, they thought, trapped in the body of a boy, was the future of football.

Garry Linnell, leading Melbourne sports writer, now deputy editor of the *Sunday Age.*

My childhood spent in Little Athletics helped my football. I am sure my high jumping was important to my marking, especially timing the leap.

# THE
# HAWTHORN
# EXPERIENCE

Marking close to the ground means you must clasp the ball strongly or it can bounce free on impact, allowing your opponent to run on to a loose ball.

By 10 I was playing in the Drouin Under 12 football team. Jim Ayres, the father of Gary Ayres, was coaching the Under 14s. In my second year I won best and fairest in the Under 12 competition and Gary finished close up in the Under 14s. He was at Hawthorn during my short stay there and now he is my coach at Geelong. Just as well we get along.

By 16 I was in the Drouin seniors playing on a wing—and at times a prayer. It was tough, compelling and unrelenting football. In one game, an older and more experienced player was giving me a wretched time, shoving and pushing, giving me an earful. Next time the ball came our way I remember seeing my brother Graham run past me and then my opponent. Only difference was when Graham left I was standing, my opponent wasn't. He was carried off. No-one came within a kilometre of me for the remainder of the match. Every now and then it didn't hurt to have your big brothers hanging about.

I played in a few country league representative matches. One was against Chelsea, who boasted a big bloke at full-forward. He was so big that when he wasn't playing footy he probably worked as an office block. It was Kevin 'Cowboy' Neale who had played 256 games with St Kilda.

Still, it was a restless time for me. Not at school and not always working, I had time on my hands. Football was a strong culture in Drouin and there was a bunch of us who were close mates. We had grown up together, played footy together at school and then with the town. We were inseparable. We weren't above grabbing a few cans and spending some evenings down at the park. One night we spotted a police car just doing its normal patrol and we panicked. I took off and jumped a fence—and landed in the largest bush of blackberries this side of the Murray. I was picking berries off me for three days and my mates were picking on me even longer.

I longed to play VFL footy after my mother took me to my first game in the big time. She was a mad South Melbourne supporter and we went to see her beloved Swans at the old Lakeside Oval. I can still picture Bobby Skilton bullocking away for the ball and the stylish Peter Bedford. The sniff of league footy was only heightened when Geoff and then Kevin joined Hawthorn.

Soon the club approached my parents seeking permission for me to play with Hawthorn. In 1979 I played six games with the reserves on permit and came back to play in Drouin's premiership side. I went back to Hawthorn in 1981. The club set me up first at a house in Kew, then Fawkner. This was a tough period for me. I don't know that I was ready for the city. I would open the door of the house, look out and feel hemmed in. The big spaces of the country were where my heart was. It was made worse because I lacked confidence.

I really didn't feel that I was a good enough footballer to be

**(opposite) Don't have to say much here. We have lost and Chris Langford celebrates Hawthorn's win in the 1989 Grand Final.**
**(below) Photographers are always looking for a different angle. Here they have excelled themselves as I pose with 1995 co-captains Ken Hinkley and Barry Stoneham.**

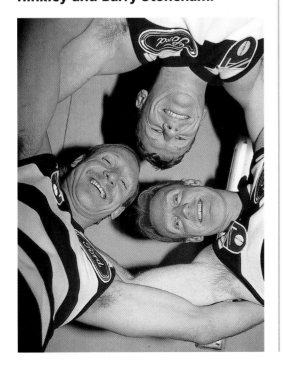

I can still see the ball tumbling towards me in slow motion and landing in my hands just before the siren to end the 1994 Preliminary Final against North Melbourne. I scored the goal to push us into the Grand Final. From left: Liam Pickering, Paul Brown and Leigh Tudor.

**(right)** I managed to bring this ball down with me after leaping over Collingwood's Gary Pert in Round seven, 1994. I landed on my back. And, yes, it hurt.

**(opposite)** Gloves can help the ball stick to your hands. But that is not much use when you release the ball on to your boot, kicking for goal. Most players take off a glove when taking a set shot.

mixing it with Leigh Matthews and Alan Martello. These blokes had been my heroes.

Every game I played in the street at Drouin with those scruffy old footballs I mimicked Matthews. I wore a Hawthorn jumper. I loved everything he did. I was determined to be like him.

The coach at Hawthorn was Allan Jeans and he was a great one—his record proves that with premierships at St Kilda (1) and Hawthorn (3). He was strong and demanded strict discipline. You either did it his way or you didn't do it at all.

There is no doubt I was uncomfortable in Melbourne. I am not sure Allan made every effort to get to know me, or work out what my problems were. I was looking for someone to settle me down and ease my mind. In 1982 I played six games but I was yet to be won over by Hawthorn or the city. At the end of the season I had had enough.

On a drive to Myrtleford to see a relative—Len Ablett, my father's cousin who played 70 games with Richmond and the mighty Jack Dyer during the war years—I made a decision that would have enormous ramifications for me.

At Myrtleford, up in the centre of Victoria, I suddenly found

Sometimes I prefer not to use gloves when conditions are perfect. In the 1994 Grand Final I opted to go gloveless to get a better feel for the footy.

myself at ease, relaxed. There were none of the pressures that had begun to haunt me in the rush and dash of city life in Melbourne. Len Ablett was with the footy club and asked if I wanted to play with the town's footy side. I said yes in an instant.

It was not a difficult decision. I was 20 and maturing, accepting that the time was coming to ensure that I had a future. I knew that I had to take a grip on my life and start to shape it the way I wanted it to go. I wasn't happy at Hawthorn, I didn't feel going back to Drouin was an option because back home it would have been easy to fall into old habits. I needed to start afresh.

This was a critical time in my life. I loved Myrtleford, the town, its people. I felt at home. The footy team had picked a few good players the season I arrived and we began to win more than the odd game. The farmers began to come to town to watch our matches. You could feel the spirit of the place lift as the team marched on.

We got to the preliminary final, pushed to a lead of 11 points with barely four minutes to go when our wingman Robbie Wright and his opponent began niggling each other. Suddenly, it escalated from two players taking each other on to a brawl. One spectator ran on and clocked Wright and put him out of business. You can imagine the mad scenes that followed. Suddenly everybody was on the field and the match stopped. I had the good sense, thankfully, to stay on the outskirts of this madness. The game was restarted but Myrtleford had lost its momentum. We were overrun.

The coach of Myrtleford, Greg Nicholls, who had played one game with Geelong in 1979, rang Bill McMaster at Geelong and said he had a player worth having a look at. It was me. So the Geelong troops came up to watch me play. By the end of the night it was decided that I would go to Geelong the following season but that I needed a clearance from Hawthorn.

So next summer I went to Geelong and immediately felt at ease in the environment. It wasn't country but it wasn't city either. I showed some good form in practice matches so Geelong went to Hawthorn for my clearance. The Hawks wouldn't budge and the matter was resolved by the Appeals Tribunal. Hawthorn, represented by Allan Jeans and others, argued that I was that club's player and that they believed I had a future in football. Geelong's argument ran along the lines that here was a young man who had tried city life once, struggled to adapt, and that Geelong would be the perfect environment.

As well, even though I knew Geelong's lifestyle would suit me, I felt that I had matured enough to make a good fist of things back in Melbourne with Hawthorn. The tribunal ruled in favor of Geelong. Hawthorn received $60,000 for my transfer and a new stage of my life was to take off.

During that summer I returned to Drouin before permanently

**(top) Teammate Mark Jackson—he played 31 games for the Cats—lends invaluable support as I fly for this mark against Footscray.**
**(above) Geelong supporters are enthusiastic and loyal. Fans wave a banner the day I reached 100 goals against North Melbourne in Round 20, 1994.**

39

**(below) It is never much fun watching from the sidelines. Injured against Fremantle in Round 19, 1995, I look on grimly.**

**(opposite) Collingwood s Gary Pert was a tough and physical opponent. He was always hard to beat, though it doesn t help when you close your eyes.**

settling back near Geelong. I remember playing a soccer match for Drouin against Moe. My mate was the goalie and he asked if I could help out. What follows is proof that you can't just pick one sport up and be at home with its rules and different rhythms.

The opposition took a corner kick, a player ran in to head the ball towards the goal and I reacted instinctively like any Aussie Rules player would. I ran straight through him. I took him out. If I described the scenes that followed as bedlam, mayhem or catastrophic then I am guilty of playing down the incident. Had there been some rope handy I would have been lynched. The opposition players were indignant, the supporters irate. They jumped out of their cars and threatened all sorts of undesirable things. Just as they ran on to the field waving their fists in anger, I concluded that I might stick to Australian Rules.

I reckon I have a good case for a free kick in this contest against Footscray. Of course, I could be bungee jumping.

To me his advantage is his combination of skill, strength, balance and ability to read the play. His overall package—a one-off gift. He can outleap, outmark and outsprint anyone, as well as outkick the best from a distance, an angle, with either foot, or any style of kick you wish to nominate. There have been footballers his equal in individual areas, but no player has been able to do it all like Ablett. His power to leap, sprint and kick long is due to the abundance and efficiency of the fast-twitch fibre portion of his muscles. Something he almost unknowingly works on with his tendency to do short-burst power training.

But his hand–eye coordination is the mystery. His level of pure ball skill should be achieved with repetitious practice as a child, continued through teenage years and adulthood. Ablett maintains them with a very limited training programme.

Dwayne Russell, journalist and broadcaster who played 50 games alongside Gary Ablett with Geelong.

43

# GEELONG: THE EARLY YEARS

I have always kept myself at arm's
length from club politics. It was a tactic
that didn't hurt on the field either.

45

(opposite) Michael Mansfield and I celebrate the last-kick win in the 1994 Preliminary Final against North Melbourne. We felt it gave us the momentum to grab the flag. West Coast thought otherwise.
(above right) Round 17, 1995, and the scoreboard notes my 100th goal.
(above) Sometimes teammates can set up play so you can do things on your head. It doesn't always work.

My League football career restarted at Geelong without trauma. I slipped down from Myrtleford and joined pre-season training under Tom Hafey, who was in his second year as coach. The club had finished a disappointing ninth under Hafey in his first year but the expectations were high for a big year in 1984. Brilliant wingman Michael Turner was in his first season as captain.

Geelong were more than happy with my form in the practice matches—too happy, in fact. It was decided that I miss a couple of practice games in case my good form became too well known and the price of my transfer fee would sky-rocket. It was an old ploy used by clubs. They often 'hid' players to keep opposition clubs out of the picture.

Importantly, I felt comfortable with Hafey. He was flexible and did not treat everyone the same. I moved to a house at Jan Juc, a surf beach not far down the coast from Geelong. The beach life was good and I enjoyed surf fishing until I found it too hard to catch anything.

I worked with the Bellarine Council on the foreshore. Work included erosion prevention and maintenance of beach facilities. It was outdoors and relaxing. Really, it was a perfect environment for a boy from the bush. Under Hafey pre-season was tough—a world apart from football at Myrtleford—but I surprised myself with the way I settled in and handled the extra training. It was a happy club and if there was any trouble about I didn't always know about it. I minded my own business.

I was on a one-year contract—perhaps my track record suggested Geelong take it one year at a time to start with—and I received about $1000 a senior game.

The first match of the season was against Fitzroy at Kardinia Park. We bolted in by 49 points and I had a good day on the wing until I collided with Garry Wilson half-way through the last quarter. I was reported for striking the great Fitzroy rover with an elbow to

47

An easy goal can see the opposition spirit drop. Here, a simple shot from the goalsquare has the Tigers worrying.

49

(above) This is not the recommended way to enjoy a Coke, but teammate Andrew Bews and David Cameron celebrate a victory in 1989.

(right) In 1995 I enjoyed the opportunity to share the captaincy with Barry Stoneham and Ken Hinkley.

(opposite) Cooperation on the forward line is imperative. Here, teammate Paul Brown makes way for me.

the head. I felt the incident looked worse than it was. Unfortunately, the VFL Tribunal, the League's disciplinary body, didn't and suspended me for three weeks. I still think it was a tough decision on a kid playing just his seventh game of League footy and coming back to the game from a season off.

I played most of the year on the wing, I had Greg Williams in the centre and Turner on the other wing. After nine games that season I was picked in the Victorian team to play Western Australia. It caused a lot of controversy because it was a big honour for a player who had just 15 League games (six at Hawthorn) under his belt. It is fair to say most felt my elevation had come too soon.

I don't think Allan Jeans—my old Hawthorn coach and also coach of the State side—was that keen to have me on board. But the great Ted Whitten stuck by me. He guaranteed that I would play well. Obviously, I was very grateful for his support then, and for the rest of my career. We lost by four points but I had a good game on the half-forward flank. I booted 8.3 and was named best for Victoria.

I ended up playing 15 games that year for Geelong and kicked 33 goals. The club voted me the best and fairest for the year—a great honour in just my second taste of League football. We finished sixth, missing the final five on percentage. We had a chance to play in the finals if we could beat defending premier Hawthorn in the last game of the season. A scoreless third quarter

Former Swan Shane Morwood became one of the League's best defenders when he played for Collingwood in 1983. We had many memorable duels.

put paid to our chances and we lost by 69 points.

My football had improved significantly, and I loved the challenge of playing with and against the best players in the country. At the end of the year I renegotiated a three-year contract for considerably more than I was on before. I can remember thinking it was big money then but football salaries have exploded. According to the AFL there was just one player earning $100,000 in 1989 and in 1995 there were 100. Now, that's big bikkies. However, it is as much an industry as a sport and players are as much entertainers as they are footballers. When TV rights are sold for $120 million and the AFL annual turnover is more than $60 million, the players deserve their fair slice of the pie.

Hafey was in his last year at Geelong in 1985 and so was Williams. He won the best and fairest but went to Sydney the following year and collected the first of his two Brownlow Medals. Geelong finished sixth again, six points shy of the final five.

Hafey and later John Devine, his replacement, used me up forward a bit more, though I felt best playing in the centre. I headed the goal-kicking list for the next two years. What I remember most about those early years at Geelong was that I was finally content in football surroundings and that I was remarkably injury free. I didn't even know what an injury was and I felt I could almost play football on consecutive days such was my ability to recover from the rigours of matches. These days I take a little longer to recover.

**(above) Concentration is the key as I prepare to snap for goal on my left foot.**
**(below) I love all sport and it was a marvellous thrill when Rugby Union champion David Campese joined in for a training run in 1994.**

The switch to full-forward was not greeted with unbridled enthusiasm when I raised it with him. He had tapered right off in the second half of 1992 as he alternated between midfield and a forward flank. The club needed a full season from Ablett and, to his credit, he slowly warmed to the idea of being the focus of the forward line at Geelong.

He had taken West Coast apart with five goals and almost 40 touches out of the middle, so the urge to get down the field and run around was still very much present. But as the goals started flowing, he became very comfortable with life in the goal square.

Longevity in our game is the hallmark of greatness. Ablett, with a contract binding him for another couple of years, will at least play until he is 37. To think he is a relative newcomer to full-forward, with three full seasons there and continuing to improve, must be a daunting prospect for opposition clubs.

Malcolm Blight, Geelong coach 1989–1994.

The 1994 Grand Final was a debacle. We lost to West Coast by 80 points. I kicked one goal and struggled to break away from Eagle fullback Michael Brennan.

# LIFE AWAY FROM FOOTBALL

**Ablett of Arabia.** The holiday to the Giza pyramids and Sphinx was a wonderful experience. I have enjoyed travelling, especially to Egypt where you come face to face with history.

**W**hen you are young, relaxation means more sport, more activity. To get a break from football, you played cricket. To get a break from cricket, you played tennis. To get a break from sport, you went rabbiting. You only stopped when you fell asleep through exhaustion.

As you grow older, relaxation takes on a less physical aspect. It is a matter of pacing yourself. I'm more likely now to sit down and read a book rather than tear around a tennis court. And I have the travel bug.

I still play backyard cricket, but this time it's not with my brothers and mates but with my children—Natasha, 13, Gary junior, 11, Nathan, 10, and Alisha, 8—and their friends. Our games are beginning to draw the kids from around the neighborhood.

Life is different from Drouin. For instance Gary junior plays in three basketball teams and Nathan two. Gary's favourite players are Michael Jordan and Andrew Gaze, while Nathan's hero is Shaquille O'Neal. Back at Drouin we played a lot of sports but basketball was not one of them. It just shows how that sport has taken off. I've played the game a bit now but I always find myself in foul trouble rather quickly. I must stop tackling.

I still like to hunt and that is despite a frightening incident in 1993 when I went shooting wild pigs with two mates. We set out on the hunt on a huge property in Balranald, NSW. The Murray was flooded and about 60 per cent of the land was under water. We left about 1 pm and stalked the pigs going upwind.

We had some success and about 4 pm decided to head back home. I had shot one boar with reasonably big tusks and threw him over my shoulder to bring back as a prize. Unfortunately, we got lost and ended up a kilometre downstream from where we had entered. We were totally unprepared. We had no matches, no lights. I climbed a tree to get our bearings but there was just water everywhere. There were only three bullets left and I had arranged with the owner of the property that if we got into trouble I would fire off three shots. So I loaded the Winchester 270 and shot off the last of our ammunition. There was no reaction. We later discovered the farmer had gone out.

That night was a full moon and we decided to try to walk out but it was difficult, wading through water that was sometimes up to our chests. Worse, just 15 minutes later the first of four thunderstorms came crashing through. They brought a freezing wind. We found some dry ground under a tree—a great place to plonk yourself in a lightning storm—to wait until dawn. But by 2.30 am we were in big trouble. One friend was dry-retching, shaking uncontrollably and struggling to breathe as the cold set in. I honestly thought we were going to lose him. I could not stop my

**(opposite) Round six, 1993, was a memorable match. Caught here between Essendon's Gavin Wanganeen and Mark Harvey, I was fortunate enough to kick 14 goals and Paul Salmon kicked 10 for the Bombers. Essendon won the match and later the Premiership.**
**(below) One hundred goals up in 1994 and the crowd was out in force. The AFL wants to keep the crowd from running on to the ground. It will be a tough task.**

(opposite, top left) The family had a great break when I took the kids up North for some football clinics. Sons Nathan and Gary show the spoils of fishing off Bathurst Island.

(opposite, middle) The two Garys and a collection of wild pigs killed in Northern Victoria.

(opposite, bottom) Much of my time away from football is spent doing promotions. Here I am on the job with racing car driver Peter Brock and Olympian ski star Kirsty Marshall.

(centre) Not just another game under lights at the MCG. It was one of the big thrills in my life playing in the Dean Jones Testimonial Match.

(above right) Son Gary takes over keeping duties in a game of backyard cricket.

knees from shaking. We had no alternative but to hug each other to keep warm and stay alive.

By dawn we had dried out a little and set about trying to find our way out. But it meant walking back through the water. By 10 am we had walked or waded probably four kilometres but remained hopelessly lost. Then we heard a gun shot. We heard it again and it was closer. We started to yell. It was the owner of the property. We were saved.

You would have thought that incident would have put me off anything to do with water. It hasn't. A neighbour has introduced me to scuba diving and I love it. To strap the tanks on and sink down underwater is a great experience. You leave the world behind. Initially I was concerned about sharks but my friend told me not to worry. 'If one is going to get you then you won't see it coming.' I think it was meant as reassurance.

So life is very different from Drouin. I still relax with children but they are my own—well, most of the time it's relaxing. I read a lot, like to watch films with the kids and have friends around to sit and chat.

Football has given me great opportunities to travel and to

The quiet before the storm. It's the singing of the national anthem before the 1994 Grand Final. Within minutes the sides will be at war.

(above) Healthy start to the day. Breakfast at the Abletts.
(below) Luxor is an ancient city on the Nile river. Here, I pose with one of the boatmen who ferried us about. You can tell he was an interesting character.
(opposite) The John Coleman Medal is awarded to the player who tops the goal-kicking list after the home-and-away games. I have been honoured to win it three times. Coleman was one of the game's greatest full-forwards.

experience history. In 1989 Geelong was involved in some exhibition games in Canada and on the way back home I stopped in London. Life in England's capital is slightly busier than Drouin. Travelling teaches you just how young a country Australia is. Here we see a tombstone dated 1805 and we think that is old. In Scotland we walked around a castle that was built in the 12th century.

The greatest experience was a trip to Egypt in 1994. It was everything I expected it to be. We visited the Giza pyramids, royal tombs built as long ago as 2700 BC; the Egyptian Museum in Cairo, which has the fabulous treasures from the tomb of Tutankhamun; the Valley of the Kings, the burial ground of Egyptian kings from around 1570 BC; the Step Pyramid at Saqqara. I rode a camel through the Sahara Desert to the Giza pyramids, which was both fascinating and dangerous. There is much archaeological work going on and the digs are guarded because of the great riches they may hold. In my haste to see the pyramids and the Great Sphinx at Giza before it grew dark I rode ahead of our tourist group. I must have gone too close to one of the digs and suddenly I had two guards by my side. Stephen Silvagni never marked me so closely.

While modern Australia is young it is, of course, the ancient home of our Aboriginal people, who have given so much to our football. I went on a week-long coaching trip up north with my two boys in 1993. It was a great experience for all of us.

I coached in Darwin and on Bathurst Island. We went pig shooting but I was more worried about crocodiles. As we moved about the small streams and rivers I kept my head down, making sure I did not mistake the back of a croc for a rock. It was much more relaxing catching barramundi. We were about to head home from Darwin when my manager rang and asked if I could I stop off at Alice Springs and do a clinic at a place called Finke. Not a problem. At Alice Springs airport we were met by a man who asked if I was Gary Ablett. He said we were in a rush because we faced a four-hour drive. Finke, we quickly found out, was not a suburb of Alice Springs. It is a small Aboriginal settlement south of Alice Springs near the South Australian border.

When we arrived we were taken to a small oval where the locals held an opening ceremony and unveiled a plaque that said The Gary Ablett Oval. I was very touched. We did the clinic and stayed the night. It was fantastic.

Even after another Grand Final loss, our supporters never lose their enthusiasm. After our poor showing against Carlton in the 1995 Grand Final the fans lined up for autographs at Kardinia Park the following day.

Gary is very much a country boy at heart and loves nothing better than a bit of pig or rabbit shooting in the off-season to get away from the hustle and bustle of being an AFL superstar. People often ask me what is Gary like? Gazza is really just your average bloke, contrary to what most people think. He talks to anyone who wants to have a chat and mixes well socially. The Geelong Football Club is very much part of his life and he has many friends there. He loves sharing a joke with the boys. And he can take one, too.

One thing a lot of people don't see is all the community work Gazza does—whether it be hospitals or nursing homes. He is very good with disabled children.

Billy Brownless, Geelong veteran of 196 games.

# THE
# COACHES

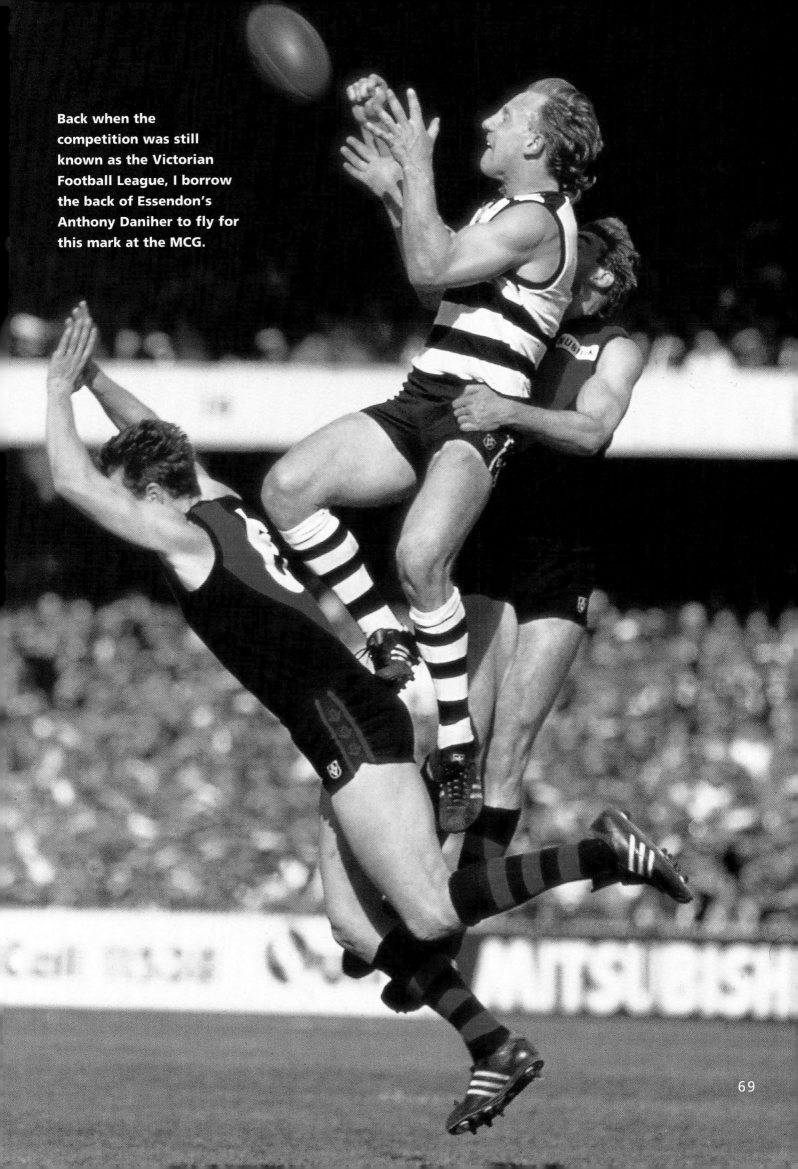

Back when the competition was still known as the Victorian Football League, I borrow the back of Essendon's Anthony Daniher to fly for this mark at the MCG.

Malcolm Blight was the best coach I have played under. That's not to criticise Gary Ayres because he is just in his second year this season at Geelong. Ayres was at Hawthorn during that club's extraordinarily successful period. Success breeds success. I have no doubt he will lead Geelong to some very significant achievements.

But Blighty coached Geelong for six years and he was outstanding. He had command over every important aspect of coaching. He was a superior tactician, his preparation was professional and diligent, his player management excellent, his knowledge of the game outstanding and his ability to impart that knowledge—from roving to rucking to defending—exceptional. I reckon he was as close as you can get to the complete coach.

When he decided to quit after the 1994 Grand Final debacle I sought him out to shake his hand. I said I was genuinely sorry that he had decided he could not go on any more. People always say that players bond through their actions on the field but players also bond with their coaches. I had enormous respect for Blight.

When he arrived at Geelong he came with a reputation as a great player—he won the 1978 Brownlow Medal with North Melbourne—and as an innovative coach—he took perennial losers Woodville to success in South Australia. For these reasons he had the Geelong players' respect from the start.

71

The Cats may not have made the Grand
Final in 1993 but I still got to run a lap of
honour on that great day. It was the first
of my three John Coleman Medals.

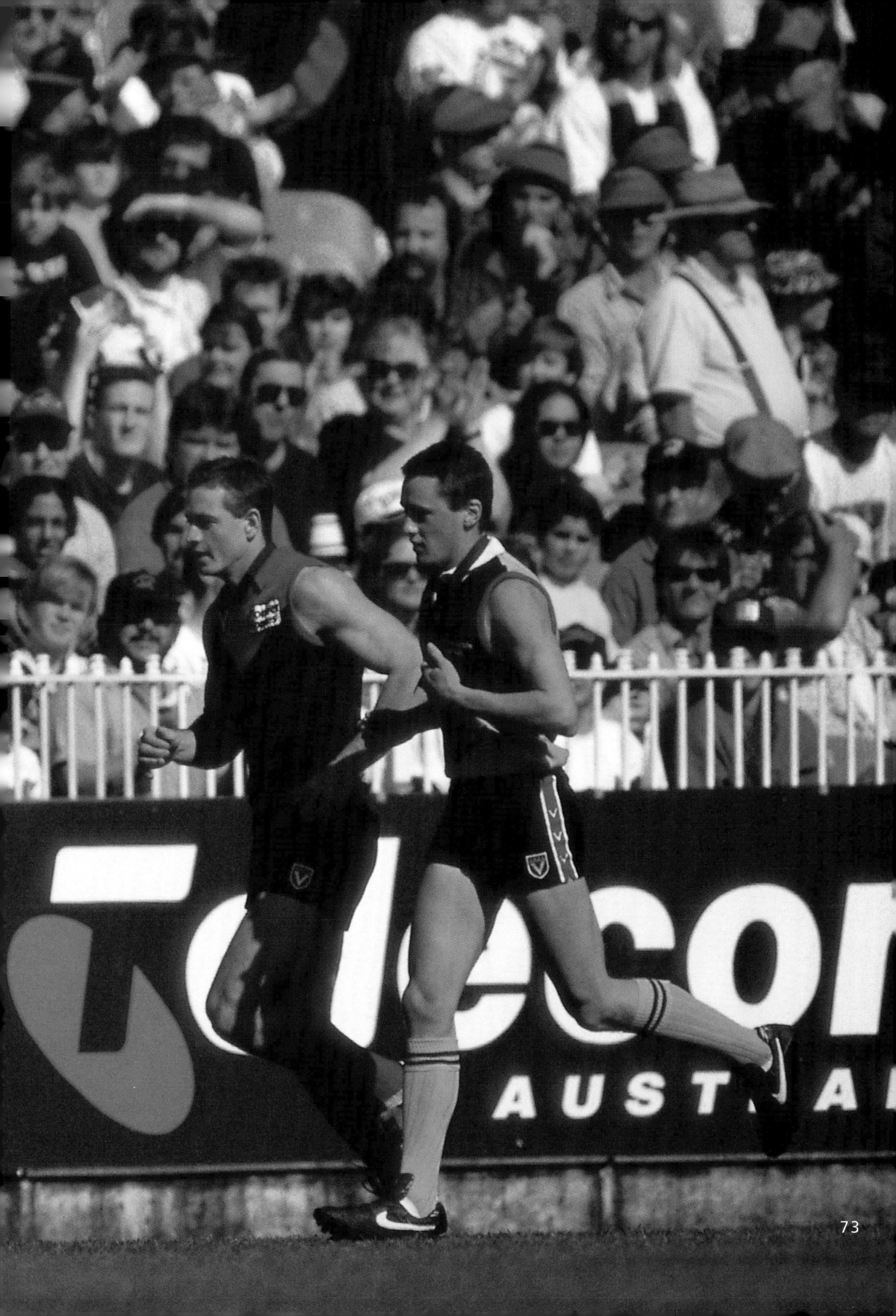

**(right)** This is a good study of two players positioning themselves. Note how both Carlton's Mil Hanna and I have our eyes on the ball.
**(below)** You can't beat winning. Robert Scott and I enjoy the moment in the rooms after another triumph.
**(opposite)** Finals fever engulfs Geelong come finals time. Enormous crowds turn out to watch us train in September.

It was Blighty who told me in 1993 that I was to play permanent full-forward. I was 31 and not getting any quicker but I loved the freedom, the space of playing upfield. I had never envisaged myself as a permanent full-forward.

But Blight worked with me, taught me a few tricks about playing the position and after four or five games I wished I had been moved there sooner in my career.

And as I said earlier Blight was innovative. Against Hawthorn one day Jason Dunstall was playing brilliantly and had booted nine goals before three-quarter time. I had snagged just two. Out came the runner and said: 'You are to go down to fullback. You are on Dunstall.' My reaction was one of disbelief. I had never played fullback and never wanted to. Certainly not on Dunstall when he was on fire. I asked the runner if he was serious. 'Yes. You are fullback.' Well, I followed instructions, but I don't know whether anyone has moved more slowly from full-forward to fullback as I did that day.

My first coach at Geelong was Tom Hafey and I liked him immediately. He was a player's man and he befriended me. I still see him quite often. He definitely was one of the reasons I settled in so easily in my second stint at AFL football.

He was tough on the track—at one practice I thought we were half-way through the session only to find out we were half-way

The Cats had the better of Footscray in 1994, even beating the Bulldogs after the siren in the first week of the finals. In this picture I just beat the spoiling Footscray defence.

through the warm-up. He was quite a good motivator and managed to get the best out of his players because he treated them as individuals.

Perhaps his greatest strength was his calmness—he never panicked, always remained cool. He was criticised for leaving struggling players in their positions too long. But he was loath to move players because he had great belief in them. I think it worked for him more than it did against him. Towards the end of his stint at Geelong there were mutterings from among some players and officials that he had not got the best out of the team. I had nothing to do with the rumblings. Hafey had been good to me.

Hafey made way for John Devine, a famous and fierce half-back flanker who played with the Cats in the 1960s. A member of the 1963 premiership side, all Devine ever wanted was success for his club. But our relationship was uneasy at times. John treated everybody the same. One in, all in. He was a strong, tough person who found it hard to make allowances for different personalities.

I have no doubt he believed in me as a player—perhaps too much. He had very high expectations of me and when I did not always realise them sometimes, I felt John thought it was because I wasn't trying. He almost took it personally if I did not play at my best.

**(below) To play for Victoria is a great honour. You get to represent your state and play with champions like Tony Lockett.**
**(bottom) I managed to play 22 games in 1995 and was relatively injury-free. Here, I stretch the hamstrings with club physiotherapist Jeff Oxley and property steward, and my old mate, Eric Gaynor.**

There hasn't been a full-forward in the game who so consistently gathers possessions. There hasn't been a modern full-forward of his stature, either. He stands 185 centimetres, the same measure as Richmond's Duncan Kellaway, yet he runs quicker and marks higher than anyone else we have seen in his role. He has the agility of a cat and the strength of a bull.

My indelible memories of him feature two games above the rest: his first appearance for Victoria (v. Western Australia in Perth in 1984) and his display in the preliminary final against Essendon at Waverley Park in 1989, the week before he was to win the Norm Smith.

He rekindled memories of the best of Alex Jesaulenko in the state game in 1984, kicking 8.3 from a half-forward flank in a losing Victorian team after just 15 games at AFL level. A few of us are embarrassed to admit we believed he had received his State jumper too soon, but his performance in Perth was astonishing. It seemed there was no limit to how high he would jump or how far he would kick. Even that master of conservatism, Allan Jeans, who coached Victoria that day, was moved to acknowledge a very solid performance.

Michael Sheahan, chief football writer with the *Herald-Sun* in Melbourne.

Teammates can help you out in marking contests. Stephen O'Reilly keeps our Richmond opponents off balance in this 1993 contest.

# THE
# FINALS

A lot of effort from four players ends in little result except for a rather symmetrical and balletic picture in this Collingwood–Geelong clash in 1994.

81

Lots of things bond teams. Coaches often take players on gruelling camps preseason. Former Footscray coach Terry Wheeler even took his men parachute jumping. At Geelong, we find a goal can do the trick.

Grand final losses haunt Geelong supporters and the players. In 1989 we lost by just six points to Hawthorn, by 28 points to West Coast in 1992, by 80 points to West Coast two years later and then by 61 points to Carlton in 1995. We have not won a flag since 1963. A drought of 32 years brings enormous pressures and four Grand Final losses in seven years only increases the burden.

There is no doubt that the loss to Carlton was the most disappointing. I felt it was our best chance of all four Grand Finals. In round 12 we got to within three points of the Blues after a sluggish start. We felt they were vulnerable.

But the early signs were not good and though you endeavour to stay positive, Carlton's early momentum proved impossible to stop. Down by seven goals at half-time and 10 at three-quarter time victory was beyond us.

At half-time Ayres demanded that we tighten up on our opponents; that we give them nowhere to run. We needed to claw our way back into the game. We knew only too well that whatever happened in the first half can be reversed in the second. In one game in 1989 we led Hawthorn by more than 50 points early in the third quarter—and lost.

I had no injury problems and felt confident before the 1995 final. I missed two opportunities early; one was a set shot from 30 metres out and another was a snap over the shoulder. Both were very gettable. Who knows what would have happened had I nailed them. The rhythm of the match may have changed completely.

While I was happy with my preparation, and coach Gary Ayres was sure he had everything spot-on and that we were primed to win, our two previous finals games may have been our undoing. In the third qualifying final we beat Footscray by 82 points. Then, in the first preliminary final we beat Richmond by 89 points. Maybe

**(above) Full-forward play is often tough man-on-man body work. As fullbacks go, there are not many stronger than North Melbourne's Mick Martyn.**
**(left) The media went to extremes to document my 100th goal in Round 17 of the 1995 season. They even took a picture of the goal umpire waving the flags.**

(top) A fan gets into the spirit of the 1994 Grand Final. Whoever did his make-up should be grateful I wear number 5 and not Justin Madden's number 44.

(above) It is one of the most famous stadiums in the world. Three Abletts together on the MCG – Garys, old and young, and Nathan.

(right) I felt 1995 was our best chance to win a Grand Final. We looked great until we fell at the very last hurdle.

we were just a little underdone both mentally and physically from not having more fierce competition in the run to the Grand Final.

I struggled to get into the game. I did not kick a goal and Stephen Silvagni played well on me. The whole club felt devastated afterwards. I had not experienced such a deep sense of disappointment before.

Our losses in 1992 and 1994 were awful experiences but West Coast was a superior side in those years. I am not so sure Carlton was in 1995, though the Blues clearly played better than us in that Grand Final.

The finals series in 1994 must go down as one of the most exciting in the history of Australian football. Billy Brownless kicked a goal after the siren to win our first qualifying final against Footscray. Badly undermanned, we beat favourites Carlton in the second semi-final, and then in the first night preliminary final in the League's history we won after the final siren again when the ball fell into my hands with four seconds to go and the scores tied.

I had been involved in a tough battle with North Melbourne's fullback Mick Martyn. It had been an engrossing match all night and with four seconds left the ball was deep in our attack. Leigh Tudor grabbed the ball right on the boundary in the forward pocket and centred the ball on his left foot.

Right then, the game seemed to go into slow motion for me. I was behind Martyn right in front of goal and I saw the ball slowly tumbling towards me until it fell into my hands. It is almost as though I looked at the ball in my hands and said 'What's this?' It was quite a bizarre feeling and an incident that took nothing more than a couple of seconds seemed to last forever. I think it went

**(opposite) Just how you like them. Passes arriving out in front of the body with the defence nowhere to be seen.**
**(above) Tom Hafey once said that coaches feel the pain of losing long after the players. However, there is no doubt losing a Grand Final burns the players very deeply.**

**(above) After our dismal showing against Carlton in the 1995 Grand Final, I still got to stand on the dais after the game to accept the John Coleman Medal.**
**(opposite) Officials are becoming more and more concerned about the injury toll in AFL football. You can see the stress and strain we put on our joints even in the act of kicking.**

much quicker for Mick Martyn.

Once I had the ball my only thoughts were to score—anything, a point, a goal. It didn't matter for the scores were tied. My only concern was not to kick into the man on the mark, though several team-mates screamed at me not to play on because the siren had gone. It was a most unlikely scenario given that I was just three metres out.

We were on a roll that final series with all the breaks going our way but even then I knew we would have to be at our very best to beat West Coast in the Grand Final. The Eagles that year had strength and skill in every position. You could not point to one particular area on the ground and find a weakness. We may have been on a roll but it was West Coast that rolled us. I managed just one goal on Michael Brennan.

In the 1992 second semi-final against West Coast I felt that we were on the verge of winning and moving straight into the Grand Final. That would have given us a much better chance of winning.

West Coast was on top of us into the third quarter of that second semi-final, but Malcolm Blight moved me from the half-forward flank to full-forward. I got the ball but not the goals, kicking 1.4 for the quarter. Had I kicked straighter I'm sure we would have won because we had the feeling the game was turning our way; we could feel the mood of the game swing.

The 1989 Grand Final loss was a different sort of disappointment. Hawthorn of that year was one of the great sides of the modern era and very few people expected us to win. The Hawks had finished 12 points ahead of us on the ladder. In the other finals we had great expectations. Not in this one. Hawthorn boasted five players—my brother-in-law Michael Tuck, Dermott Brereton, Gary Ayres (now Geelong coach), Chris Mew and Bertie DiPierdomenico playing in their seventh consecutive Grand Final sides.

In that year my focus was as good as it has ever been. I was in nice touch, kicking 8.5 in the preliminary final against Essendon. In the Grand Final Hawthorn started Scott Maginness on me but he was shifted after I had kicked four goals, 12 minutes into the second quarter. I played the rest of the game on Chris Langford and finished with 9.1.

With such an experienced line-up Hawthorn was least affected by nerves in front of the crowd of 94,796 people and quickly took a solid lead. The Hawks appeared to have the game under control at three-quarter time.

That we fought back to go down by just one goal was a turning point for the club. Geelong had a reputation as a side that could not summon the strength and willpower to fight back, especially in critical games. Hawthorn had one of the best sides they have had in 20 years. To do that against Hawthorn was an extraordinary achievement.

The Grand Final parade through the middle of
Melbourne the day before the Grand Final is
tough on the players, but up to 70,000 fans
crowd the streets to watch.

Back in Geelong that night, thousands waited outside City Hall to applaud the players, not only for making the Grand Final but also for their efforts throughout the season.

It had, of course, been topped off on an individual basis by Paul Couch winning the Brownlow Medal and Ablett being named as the Norm Smith medallist after kicking 9.1 in the premiership decider. The club asked me to introduce coach Malcolm Blight and the players and I brought them on-stage in ascending numerical order, except for Couch and Ablett, who were saved till last. The public address system was cranked up to rival a Rolling Stones concert, but when it came to saying 'the Norm Smith medallist ... Gary Ablett' I couldn't hear myself speak. The crowd went mad and the noise was ear-shattering.

Ian Cover, journalist, broadcaster and member of the Coodabeen Champions and now Member of Parliament.

# THE
# HIGHEST
# MARK

**Preliminary Final day in 1993. When Essendon staged its remarkable second-half comeback against Adelaide, I received my first John Coleman Medal.**

One of the questions I'm often asked is, how has Christianity changed my attitudes to football and life in general and 'what do I actually believe?' Well, although Christianity has changed my attitudes to life in many different areas, it is impossible for me to express all that I believe in a single chapter. However, one area I've chosen to share is one that I believe God has been continually challenging me in. It is my hope that what I've shared will challenge you also.

'From life's outset, we find ourselves on the prowl, searching to satisfy some inner, unexplained yearning. Our hunger causes us to search for people who will love us. Our desire for acceptance pressures us to perform for the praise of others. We strive for success, driving our minds and bodies harder and farther, hoping that because of our sweat and sacrifice, others will appreciate us more.

But the man or woman who lives only for the love and attention of others is never satisfied—at least, not for long. Despite our efforts, we will never find lasting, fulfilling peace if we have to continually prove ourselves to others. Our

**(opposite) Space and loose ball on the forward line are rare commodities. You make the most of them.**
**(below) Round 17, 1993, against Collingwood. A little fine tuning before the battle commenced.**

Sean Simpson joins me in another Grand Final parade. Geelong has been in four since 1989. We hope to be in our fifth shortly, and we hope it turns into a grand celebration. My son Nathan is in the foreground.

desire to be loved and accepted is a symptom of a deeper need—the need that often governs our behaviour and is the primary source of our emotional pain. Often unrecognised, this is our need for SELF-WORTH.'

These words written by Robert S. McGee in his bestseller *The Search for Significance* pretty well sum up my own experience.

Psychologist Lawrence J. Crabb Jr, describes our need for self-esteem in this way: 'The basic personal need of each person is to regard himself as a worthwhile human being.' And, according to William Glasser, 'Everyone aspires to have a happy, successful, pleasurable belief in himself.'

Why is the need for self-worth such a powerful driving force in our lives? If we really are nothing more than animals who are only here by accident in a mindless, mechanistic universe, with no meaning, no value and no destiny, why is this cry for self-worth so dominating?

I suggest that it is because we are not here by accident—that at the back of everything is an awesome God who created everything for a purpose—with mankind being the pinnacle of his handy work, created in his own image, being of infinite worth in his sight. Since the God who is there is a God of intense intimacy we are all created for relationship, firstly with God himself and then with others.

Some secular psychologists focus on self-worth with a goal of simply feeling good about ourselves. A biblical self-concept, however, goes far beyond that limited perspective. It is an accurate perception of ourselves, God, and others, based on the truth of God's words. An accurate, biblical self-concept contains both strength and humility.

Whether we call it self-esteem or self-worth, the feeling of significance is crucial to our emotional, spiritual and social stability, and is the driving force within the human heart. Understanding our need in this area helps us to understand our actions and motivations. What a waste of time to attempt to correct behaviour without first seeking to understand the needs and motivations that cause such behaviour! Yet millions of people spend a lifetime searching for love, acceptance and success without understanding the need that drives them. We need to understand that this hunger for self-worth is God given and can only be satisfied by God himself. Our value is not dependent on our ability to perform or earn the fickle acceptance of people, but rather its true source is the unconditional love and acceptance of God. He created us. He alone knows how to fulfill all our needs.

As marvellous as it is, salvation means more than forgiveness of sins. In the same act of love through which God forgave our sins, he also provided for our righteousness: the worthiness to stand in God's presence. By imputing righteousness to us, God attributes Christ's worth to us. The moment we accept Christ, God

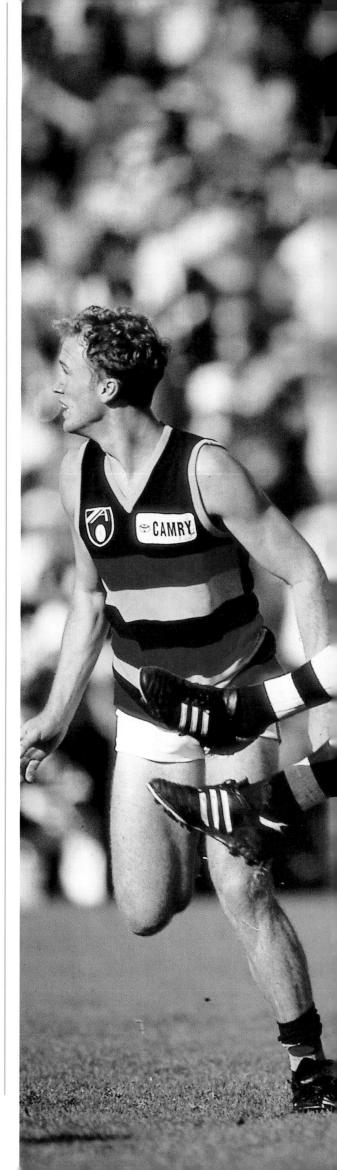

(left) In 1992 Geelong scored goals with ease. In Rounds six and seven we tallied 60 goals—32 against Adelaide and 28 against Essendon. Here, I let fly at goal with my left foot against Adelaide.

(below) There is great camaraderie in victory. We celebrate a win in 1994.

no longer sees us as condemned sinners. Instead we are forgiven, we receive Christ's righteousness, and God sees us as creatures who are fully pleasing to him.

It has taken me years to begin to realise that God doesn't determine my worth by my ability to perform. Rather, my worth is based on the fact that God came in the person of Jesus Christ and gave his life for me, and therefore imparted great value to me. The fact that God was willing to pay the ultimate price to save me from a lost eternity and bring me back into a right relationship with himself establishes my worth in his sight forever. In Christ, God has given me a secure self-worth totally apart from my ability to perform both on and off the football field, a self-worth that success cannot add to, nor can failure take away from.

One day, not so far away, I won't be able to perform on a football field. The roar of the crowd will cease, at least for me anyway. I thank God that my sense of significance is not confined to a football arena, and that his purpose for my life goes far beyond my natural abilities. I've had the thrill of taking some high marks in my career, but there is yet a higher mark, the destiny for which we are all created, to spend eternity with God and enjoy him forever. The most important decision anyone will ever make in life is what they do with Jesus Christ. Our eternal destiny depends on it.

**(above) Taking the field for the 1992 Grand Final. Twice we got four goals ahead of West Coast, but could not hold back a Peter Matera fightback.**

**(opposite, top) It's 100 goals up in 1994 and the crowd surrounds me. I kicked 129 goals for the season.**

**(opposite, bottom) Gavin Brown, Garry Lyon, Jason Dunstall, Gavin Wanganeen, Greg Williams and Stewart Loewe join me at the launch of Club 10, a promotion company established by former AFL player Ricky Nixon in 1995.**

John Paul Young's 'Love Is In The Air' has become 'Ablett's In The Air'. Silly, I know, but I like it. It's light and bubbly and basically unbelievable, but that's how it felt watching the 1989 Grand Final when Gazza single-handedly took on the might of the Hawthorn Football Club, possibly the best team in the history of the game, and nearly beat them. For anyone fortunate enough to witness that match, it remains shrouded in an aura. To recall it is to experience a pleasure like listening to music.

Martin Flanagan, renowned Melbourne journalist and author.

# THE QUIET, UNASSUMING GENIUS

**By Professor Geoffrey Blainey**

*Professor Geoffrey Blainey is a renowned historian and author with a passion for sport and especially Geelong.*

I might not look too confident, but I still mananged to haul this mark in against Melbourne in 1989.

**H**e is the most memorable of footballers but in an odd way he is often hard to remember. There is something of the will-o'-the-wisp about Ablett. He is like a vanishing trick.

It is strange that one seems to remember more vividly other champions of Geelong. I seem to see old Reg Hickey, captain and coach in the late 1930s, occasionally wearing a sleeveless guernsey, which was then uncommon, and slightly red in the face as he waits at fullback beside the goalpost at the bay end of Corio Oval. After 50 years still fresh in memory is wavy-haired Lindsay White, having led too far from goal, about to boot his long drop kick and sure to make the distance but not the six points. And Bob Davis, eternally running, is bouncing the ball with all the space in the world in front of him, running far faster than his bulky physique should have allowed.

For some reason my mind carries no set picture of Gary Ablett. Is it because he is so unpredictable? Or so versatile? No specific skill is the essence or hallmark of his game, though his high marking, being so pictorial, receives the most attention on television and radio and the back page of the papers.

You could almost say that Ablett is a combination of certain of the great players of the recent past, born again in a new body. He is a long kick but adept at that gentle, almost soccer-like shot that is new to the game. Pitted against high-markers he can soar above them. He is a master of that last second mark when the ball is just about to touch the ground. He is an exemplar of that last-minute shove in the back that used to be called illegal. He bumps with a crunch, like a barrel-chested ruckman. He is just as skilled as a small wingman in running at full pace and picking up a dribbling ball.

Few of us imagined that we would see in one player that kind of low-slung brilliance of St Kilda's Darrel Baldock, the ball always on a string when near the grass, combined with the high marking of Essendon's John Coleman, the dodging of Les Foote at Arden

(opposite) Some things went right in the 1992 Grand Final—even a one-handed mark with eyes closed—but we still lost by 28 points as West Coast won its first premiership.
(above right) One hundred goals up in 1995 and Geelong runner Phillip Walsh helps keep the fans at bay.

107

**(below) The dust and crowd settle down after notching my century of goals in 1995.**

**(opposite)  Injury has restricted me to just 11 games and 43 goals for Victoria, and that has been a great disappointment. The great Ted Whitten taught me the significance and tradition of interstate football.**

Street, and the courage of a Tony Shaw in grabbing at the bottom of a pack. Ablett is every one of them, embodied in one pair of legs and arms.

He has off days, though on some of his ordinary days he performs at least one extraordinary feat. He plays so few bad games that they too are memorable. He had a woeful day against Melbourne on a warm day at the start of—was it the 1994 season? His performance in finals since the miraculous Grand Final against Hawthorn in 1989 has been patchy.

He was sufficiently out of touch during the Grand Final against West Coast in 1994, a year in which he had risen to great heights, that at the start of the next season maybe half of the football commentators did not pick Geelong to make the final eight, let alone the final two. Their pessimism must have stemmed from the instinct, which they wisely did not emphasise in public, that Ablett had well and truly passed his prime. And yet Geelong rose again in 1995, with Ablett playing uncannily week after week. Then came the Grand Final in which, to the dismay of so many, he was not himself on the day of the year that counted. It is a sign of his status that supporters remain loyal to him.

His last three seasons have been astonishing for someone of his years. It is a feat to move to full-forward—a graveyard for cunning, fading old champions transferred from down the field— and to shine there. Furthermore, to exceed 100 goals in each season and to earn enough kicks to have reached 150 goals—if he

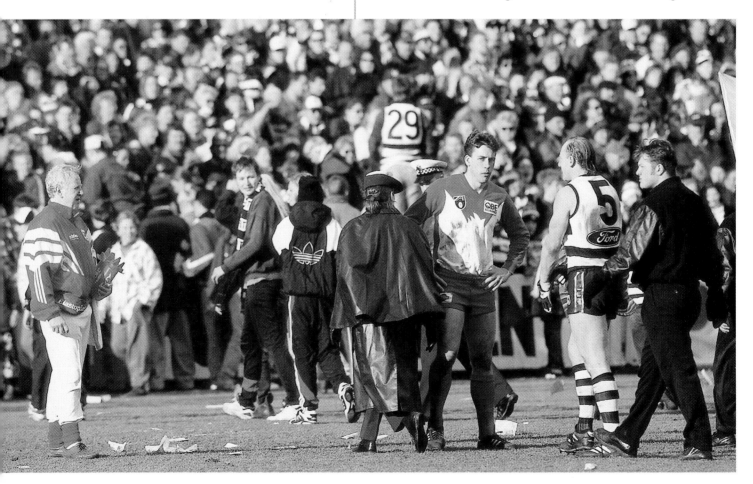

It's 1988 and Geelong teammates David Cameron and Darren Troy drink (softly) to another victory.

(opposite) Better late than never. Eyes on the ball, I prepare to ride my Footscray opponents in this 1995 match.
(right) Stephen Silvagni was a hard man to beat in the 1995 Grand Final, but this time I had a head start.

had been a straight shooter—is one of the most momentous feats in the history of the game. If the League were to award a Greater Brownlow for three successive years of rare achievement, he should win that medal.

He is unpredictable in so many ways. When he was approaching what seemed then to be the peak of his career, the Geelong club could not even feel sure whether he would bother to play any more games of senior football.

This casual characteristic is almost engaging—except to the coach. One day at Kardinia Park, I was fortunate to be invited into the players' room just before a game. There he was, merely pretending to do the warm-up exercises which all other players were doing with gusto and vigour. He was not a team man until relatively late in his career. And yet his individualism, his religious yearnings, they command respect. They distinguish him.

Curiously, on the field he does not, until the moment he performs, look like The Champion. If you were a foreign tourist in Geelong, and if you took a keen interest in a variety of sports, and if you were taken to your very first Australian football game, and if you were asked—just before the ball was bounced—which of the 36 players on the field was the acknowledged champion— no, you would probably not pick Gary Ablett. In days gone by, you might pick Jack Dyer or Ron Barassi, having observed their presence and their commanding air when they have ran on to the field. But unless you knew who Ablett was, would you pick him as the champion?

**(below) Theatre critics may accuse me of overacting as I react to this challenge from Melbourne's Matthew Febey in 1993.
(opposite) I have shared much with Billy Brownless on the Geelong forward line. He is a fine kick and strong mark. Brownless also has a great sense of humour, as viewers of _The Footy Show_ have witnessed.**

On the field he can be introspective and self-effacing. There is no swagger. At times he displays a lost-in-the-clouds look as if he does not know whether it is Saturday or Sunday. After he has brought down a remarkable mark, he is capable of breaking out into a slight smile of puzzlement or even wonderment. It is a quarter smile, no more. It goes without saying that part of his extraordinary fame comes from television and the way the camera, more than ever before, captures in slow-motion his aerobatics and his facial expression.

He has given pleasure to enormous crowds: not universal pleasure because many supporters of opposing clubs wish he did not exist. It would be hard, however, to think of any other footballer of the last 60 years who has displayed so often his mixture of skill and magic along with a strand of humility and a strand of sheer aggression.

There have been miracle players in the past. Other miracle players will come again, once in a decade, once in a quarter century. It is futile to ask who is the best footballer of all time. We should simply marvel at this phenomenon, sometimes called the 'pontiff', while he is still around.

(opposite) A tip for children. Learn
the basic techniques and practise
them and then practise them again.
As my Dad told me—learn to use
both sides of the body.
(above) After four Grand Final
losses, critics would expect us to be
down and out. But we are not.

# STATISTICS

**(provided by Col Hutchinson, AFL statistician)**

## Premiership seasons

**Geelong 1984-1995** 225 games, 952 goals

**Hawthorn 1982** 6 games, 9 goals

**TOTAL 231 961**

**Pre-season competition** 14 games, 19 goals

**State Matches** 11 games, 43 goals

**Finals matches** 15 games, 63 goals

**Grand Finals** 4 games, 13 goals

**Brownlow votes** 95 (94 Geelong, 1 Hawthorn)

**Best and Fairest Won** 1984, second 1985, 1993, 1994, 1995;
third 1986, 1989, 1990

**Captain Co-captain** 1995, 1996

**Norm Smith Medallist** (best player in Grand Final) 1989

**Coleman Medallist** (leading goal-kicker) 1993, 1994, 1995

**All Australian Team 1984**, 1989, 1990, 1992, 1993, 1994, 1995 (capt)

| Season | Team | Games | Goals |
|--------|----------|-------|-------|
| 1982 | Hawthorn | 6 | 9 |
| 1984 | Geelong | 15 | 33 |
| 1985 | Geelong | 20 | 82 |
| 1986 | Geelong | 15 | 65 |
| 1987 | Geelong | 17 | 53 |
| 1988 | Geelong | 21 | 82 |
| 1989 | Geelong | 23 | 87 |
| 1990 | Geelong | 17 | 75 |
| 1991 | Geelong | 12 | 28 |
| 1992 | Geelong | 21 | 72 |
| 1993 | Geelong | 17 | 124 |
| 1994 | Geelong | 25 | 129 |
| 1995 | Geelong | 22 | 122 |

# Where Ablett Rates

## Most Goals Round By Round

| Round 1 | Tony Modra (Adel) | 13 | v | Carlton (1994) |
|---|---|---|---|---|
| Round 2 | Doug Strang (Rich) | 14 | v | North Melb (1931) |
| Round 3 | Bob Pratt (S. Melb) | 15 | v | Essendon (1934) |
| Round 4 | Tony Lockett (St. K) | 12 | v | Melbourne (1987) |
| Round 5 | Peter Hudson (Haw) | 16 | v | Melbourne (1969) |
| Round 6 | **Gary Ablett (Geel)** | **14** | **v** | **Essendon (1993)** |
| Round 7 | Jason Dunstall (Haw) | 17 | v | Richmond (1992) |
| Round 8 | **Gary Ablett (Geel)** | **14** | **v** | **Sydney (1994)** |
| Round 9 | **Gary Ablett (Geel)** | **14** | **v** | **Richmond (1989)** |
| Round 10 | Lindsay White (Geel) | 11 | v | St Kilda (1948) |
| | **Gary Ablett (Geel)** | **11** | **v** | **Brisbane (1988)** |
| Round 11 | Gordon Coventry (Coll) | 15 | v | Essendon (1933) |
| Round 12 | Gordon Coventry (Coll) | 17 | v | Fitzroy (1930) |
| Round 13 | Gordon Coventry (Coll) | 16 | v | Hawthorn (1929) |
| Round 14 | Gordon Coventry (Coll) | 14 | v | Hawthorn (1934) |
| | John Longmire (N. Melb) | 14 | v | Melbourne (1990) |
| Round 15 | Bob Pratt (S. Melb) | 12 | v | Footscray (1934) |
| | Peter Hudson (Haw) | 12 | v | St Kilda (1971) |
| | Simon Beasley (Foots) | 12 | v | Melbourne (1985) |
| Round 16 | Tony Modra (Adel) | 13 | v | Richmond (1993) |
| Round 17 | Doug Wade (Geel) | 13 | v | S. Melbourne (1967) |
| Round 18 | John Coleman (Ess) | 13 | v | Hawthorn (1952) |
| Round 19 | Fred Fanning (Melb) | 18 | v | St Kilda (1947) |
| Round 20 | Doug Wade (Geel) | 13 | v | N. Melbourne (1971) |
| | Peter Daicos (Coll) | 13 | v | Brisbane (1991) |
| Round 21 | Tony Lockett (St K) | 13 | v | Carlton (1991) |
| Round 22 | Peter Hudson (Haw) | 11 | v | Fitzroy (1970) |
| | Jason Dunstall (Haw) | 11 | v | St Kilda (1989) |
| Round 23 | Scott Hodges (Adel) | 11 | v | Geelong (1992) |
| Round 24 | Tony Lockett (St K) | 11 | v | Sydney (1991) |

## Leading all-time goal kickers

|  | Goals | Games | Av per game |
|---|---|---|---|
| G Coventry (Coll) | 1299 | 306 | 4.25 |
| J Dunstall (Haw) | 1077 | 225 | 4.79 |
| D Wade (Geelong/N. Melb) | 1057 | 267 | 3.96 |
| T Lockett (St Kilda/Sydney) | 1008 | 202 | 4.99 |
| J Titus (Richmond) | 970 | 294 | 3.30 |
| **G Ablett (Haw-Geel)** | **961** | **231** | **4.16** |
| L Matthews (Haw) | 915 | 332 | 2.76 |
| P McKenna (Coll/Carl) | 874 | 191 | 4.58 |
| B Quinlan (Foots/Fitz) | 815 | 366 | 2.23 |
| K Bartlett (Rich) | 778 | 403 | 1.93 |

## Bags of 7 or More

|  | 17 | 16 | 15 | 14 | 13 | 12 | 11 | 10 | 9 | 8 | 7 |
|---|---|---|---|---|---|---|---|---|---|---|---|
| G Coventry (1299) | 1 | 1 | 1 | 1 | 1 | - | 5 | 2 | 11 | 16 | 25 |
| J Dunstall (1077) | 1 | - | - | - | 4 | 5 | 4 | 13 | 11 | 13 |
| D Wade (1057) | - | - | - | - | 2 | - | 2 | - | 5 | 10 | 21 |
| T Lockett (1008) | - | 1 | 1 | - | 1 | 5 | 3 | 5 | 10 | 12 | 20 |
| J Titus (970) | - | - | - | - | - | - | - | 3 | 4 | 9 | 3 |
| **G Ablett (961)** | **-** | **-** | **-** | **3** | **-** | **2** | **2** | **5** | **4** | **10** | **16** |
| L Matthews (915) | - | - | - | - | - | - | 2 | - | - | 2 | 10 |
| P McKenna (874) | - | 1 | - | - | 1 | 4 | 4 | 3 | 7 | 9 | 16 |
| B Quinlan (815) | - | - | - | - | - | - | 1 | 1 | 2 | 3 | 6 |
| K Bartlett (778) | - | - | - | - | - | - | - | - | - | 1 | 3 |

## Total of Top Individual goalkickers at Each Club

| Club | Player | Goals |
|---|---|---|
| Adelaide | Tony Modra | 262 |
| Brisbane | Roger Merrett | 147 |
| Carlton | Harry Vallence | 722 |
| Collingwood | Gordon Coventry | 1299 |
| Essendon | Simon Madden | 575 |
| Fitzroy | Jack Moriarty | 626 |
| Footscray | Simon Beasley | 575 |
| **Geelong** | **Gary Ablett** | **952** |
| Hawthorn | Jason Dunstall | 1077 |
| Melbourne | Norm Smith | 546 |
| N Melbourne | John Longmire | 494 |
| Richmond | Jack Titus | 970 |
| S. Melb/Sydney | Bob Pratt | 681 |
| St Kilda | Tony Lockett | 898 |
| West Coast | Peter Sumich | 460 |

# ACKNOWLEDGEMENTS

Photos on p.3 by Darrin Braybrook (*Sport. The Library*), p.4 by Tony Feder (*Sporting Pix*), p.5 *Sporting Pix*, p.6 Jeff Crow (*Sport. The Library*), p.7 David Callow (*Sport. The Library*), p.8 & 9 Tony Feder (*Sporting Pix*), p.10 David Callow (*Sport. The Library*), p.11 & 12 Don Lumm, p.13 Darrin Braybrook (*Sport. The Library*), p.14 *The Age*, p.15 Ray Kennedy (*The Age*), p.17 David Callow (*Sport. The Library*), p.18 Sean Garnsworthy (*Sporting Pix*), p.20 John Daniels (*Sporting Pix*), p21 *The Age*, p.22 & 23 David Callow (*Sport. The Library*), p.24 Stuart Milligan (*Sporting Pix*), p.25 Don Lumm, p.26 & 27 *The Age*, p.28 & 29 *Sporting Pix*, p.31 Darrin Braybrook (*Sport. The Library*), p.32 *The Age*, p.33 Stuart Milligan (*Sporting Pix*), p.34 & 35 John Daniels (*Sporting Pix*), p.36 Phillip Stubbs (*Sporting Pix*), p37 David Callow (*Sport. The Library*), p.38 Tony Feder (*Sporting Pix*), p.39 (top) *Sporting Pix* (bottom) Tony Feder (*Sporting Pix*), p.40 John Daniels (*Sporting Pix*), p.41 Jeff Crow (*Sport. The Library*), p.42 & 43 *The Age*, p.45 *The Age*, p.46 Darrin Braybrook (*Sport. The Library*), p.47 (left) *Sporting Pix*,(right) Tony Feder (*Sporting Pix*), p.48 & 49 *The Age*, p.50 (left) *Sporting Pix*, (right) Darrin Braybrook (*Sport. The Library*), p.51 Jeff Hogg (*Sport. The Library*), p.52 Tony Feder (*Sporting Pix*), p.53 (top) Ken Irwin (*Sport. The Library*), (bottom) Stuart Milligan (*Sporting Pix*), p.54 & 55 Darrin Braybrook (*Sport. The Library*), p.58 John Daniels (*Sporting Pix*), p.59 Martin Philbey (*Sport. The Library*), p.60 (bottom) Tony Feder (*Sporting Pix*), p.60 & 61 (centre) *The Age*, p.61 Don Lumm, p.62 & 63 Martin Philbey (*Sport. The Library*), p.64 (top) Don Lumm, p.65 *The Age*, p.66 & 67 *The Age*, p.69 Tony Feder (*Sporting Pix*), p.70 Martin Philbey (*Sport. The Library*), p.71 David Callow (*Sport. The Library*), p.72 & 73 David Callow (*Sport. The Library*), p.74 (top) David Callow (*Sport. The Library*), (bottom) *The Age*, p.75 Darrin Braybrook (*Sport. The Library*), p.76 Martin Philbey (*Sport. The Library*), p.77 (top) David Callow (*Sport. The Library*) (bottom) Jeff Crow (*Sport. The Library*), p.78 & 79 Darrin Braybrook (*Sport. The Library*), p.81 Jim Hooper (*Sport. The Library*), p.82 (*Sport. The Library*), p.83 (top) *The Age*, (bottom) Tony Feder (*Sporting Pix*), p.84 David Callow (*Sport. The Library*), p.84 & 85 Sean Garnsworthy (*Sporting Pix*), p.86 Martin Philbey (*Sport. The Library*), p.87 *The Age*, p.88 Tony Feder (*Sporting Pix*), p.89 *The Age*, p.90 & 91 David Callow (*Sport. The Library*), p.93 Tony Feder (*Sporting Pix*), p.94 *The Age*, p.95 Tony Feder (*Sporting Pix*), p.96 & 97 David Callow (*Sport. The Library*), p.98 & 99 *Sporting Pix*, p.99 Martin Philbey (*Sport. The Library*), p.100 John Krutop (*Sport. The Library*), p.101 (top) Tony Feder (*Sporting Pix*), (bottom) David Callow (*Sport. The Library*), p.102 & 103 Stuart Milligan (*Sporting Pix*), p.105 John Krutop (*Sporting Pix*), p.106 Tony Feder (*Sporting Pix*), p.107 Tony Feder (*Sporting Pix*), p.108 Darrin Braybrook (*Sport. The Library*), p.109 *The Age*, p.110 & 111 *Sporting Pix*, p.112 Sean Garnsworthy (*Sporting Pix*), p.113 Darrin Braybrook (*Sport. The Library*), p.114 David Callow (*Sport. The Library*), p.115 David Callow (*Sport. The Library*), p.116 *Sport.The Library*, p.117 Ray Kennedy (*The Age*), p.118 David Callow (*Sport. The Library*) and p.121 Martin Philbey (*Sport. The Library*).